Never Been to Berlin

Publisher: DEE ELL PUBLISHING

ISBN: 978-0-9812123-9-5

Further information: albertklassen@icloud.com

Never Been to Berlin

albert klassen

Never Been to Berlin

Books by Albert Klassen

the death of the girl with the beautiful hair
looking at life from an angle
the life of lido pepperman
the church
radical madness
a monk in paradise
the abstract god
journey
never been to berlin

Chapter One

where you goin
wid your hands in your pockets
and nothing to do
so then
how bout appropriating someone else's style
kick it up a notch
and do some cracking

share with me
share the land
give me your hand
together we walk in this barren country
with only porridge and sweet peas to eat
what happened
oh it's only a dream
such a relief

gonna buy a lobster
cook it up
dip it in butter
yes

and then around the corner we wait for the
hypocrites
come over here Mr. Hypocrite
sit down
I will cut off your hair
all of it

I can see the idols glaring at me
how dare you
we are real
we have power
we swear by heaven's name

layers upon layers of bewilderment
and in the middle a dose of religiosity
resting on the books of first and second Samuel

dance oh daughters of Sodom
prance oh harlots of Gomorrah
you get my vote
let me propose a new rule
no Molotov cocktails before noon

lonely old men shuffling up to the bar
give me a drink please

here you go
they go and sit down and drink
the lonely strippers join them
buy me a drink old man
of course
it's my duty
it's my pleasure
it's the least I can do for after all
you bared it all for me
glances are exchanged
another drink here

in another part of town the artist paints in her loft
artists love to live in lofts
it seems the right place to paint
she eats cake and washes it down with coffee
into the night she paints
while her cat lies curled up at her feet
artists need their cats
artists don't have dogs
dogs are a distraction
cats inspire

strippers are a man's best friend
they show him everything
their honesty is intoxicating
and when they catch his eye he feels wanted
respected
his bruised ego stroked
ready for another week of battle

a fragmented personal life
every day stitching everything together again
even as it falls apart
trying to find order and still it gets so confusing
where is the right tool to do the job
I thought it was there
or here
where is it

what makes you mad
or sad
and then you grab a six pack
and you feel so good
good night
in the morning you grab your head
why
why why why
please mr.musician play us a song
stroke the strings of your guitar
soothe our spirits
take us to another place
where people live with grace
where people respect your space
where people don't hate you for your race
play it again

connected and yet so far apart
ideologies stretched over thin and fragile frames
feeling the crushing weight of historical significance
that shadow that hovers above our spirits

threatening to tear us apart
showering us with sparks of disenchantment

the man in the long black coat
he's walking slowly
and as he passes the mirror at the bus stop
he stops and stares
brushing his hair slightly
cocking his head to one side
and then he's on his way
we all are on a path
a crooked path
a straight path
an uneven path
a smooth path

Chapter Two

a mouse in your house
is like having
a louse for a spouse
it's an inconvenient terror

living with depair
takes out all the air
in rooms that reek of heartache
as the stench of uncivil conversation takes over
rendering the inhabitants powerless to find joy
their brains filled with thoughts of murder and
revenge
plotting to get even
to turn the tables

to get back
and never ever to share the sack
with the one they used to love

the relevancy of your sobriety
is it in style
get it together
pass the pecans
did we remember to lock the door
I don't know

a thin blue sky
in a big fat universe
it's an artist's nightmare
and where
is our sense of humour

we stopped looking at the sky
looking for a sign
now we hide in caves
looking inside ourselves
closing our minds
shutting the door
scared of the light

jfk we heard you as you whispered
was it last Friday or
Tuesday afternoon

well I've never been to Berlin

never touched the Brandenburg gate
or walked where Adolph walked
so what
I too am a Berliner
I feel the angst and
the terror of its historical significance
as it influences our zeitgeist

Ich weiß was ich weiß
und ich weiß nichts
mein Leben ist eine Schande
tief in meine Seele weine ich
und wer wird mir retten

escaping from the reality of what we didn't achieve
when we were so close to realizing our dreams
it's a constant craving
please play me a rock and roll song
please play me an overture
please play me a lullaby
so I can cry
myself to sleep
and dream of the greatness that I craved

all the way to the SuperBowl he went
and then he lost
it was a heartbreak

I listened to all the doom and gloom
as I watched a purple flower bloom

the world around me was going insane
filled with so much hate and pain
and as I watched that flower I began to cry
thinking of all the people that wanted to die
that I was one of them was sadder still

jesus and peter walked on water
never heard of anyone else doing that
it was quite a feat
especially for pete
only did it once
and then he sank
like a rock
save me master he cried out
and the master saved him
there was something in the air those days
a revolutionary spirit was brewing
with god stirring the pot
again
and since then we've been to the moon
and dropped a few atomic bombs
and invented the Internet

we linger on
stoned weary lonely and sad
to each other
strangers
even our mirrors are fake
deception grows
truth is an absurd metaphor

like walking on water
or saying time moves in circles
it's all there
beauty and holiness and honesty and purity

I saw a grand piano floating in the ocean and it was
white
along came a pirate and sank it out of spite
then a navy ship came by and shot the pirate dead
it filled that dude with lead

in the synagogue they sang hallelujah
and passed the offering plate

I stood on the corner and listened to the violin play
it had so much to say
the strings trembled as they sang
my ears rang

it was profound and interesting
as was her face
it was a case
of mistaken identity
but she was only trying to be free
and so we sang a song of sixpence a pocket full of rye
with monks lining the street and asking us why
give us a reason
for what we asked
for painting your faces and acting so crazy
and we gave them no answer

because we didn't know
and who really does know
it's all such a mystery
what we
want to be
or become like

so put on your shorts and ride your bike
up the mountain and to the lookout
where you can mediate and find your own truth
hoping it will set you free

Chapter 3

the disco ball went round and round
it's shimmering light bouncing on the ground
where the people danced
round and round they pranced
writhing bodies in the heat
touching and groping meat on meat
moving to the pulsating beat
reaching out to meet
and greet

the ancient drumbeat calls us from our distant past
come hither maidens and lads
press your hearts against the barb wire fence and
yearn
for a spiritual encounter

and pray that the spirits will enter and engulf you
spraying their mysticism on your soul
so that you will feel the presence of God
and bow with reverence and respect
praying for the healing touch
to wipe away your pain and misery and bitterness

the soldier stood up on command and sprayed his
enemy with machine gun fire
killing and maiming in the confusion of war
and then a bullet hit him in the head
and he was dead
brought down by a piece of lead

the dreams all fell by the wayside and chatted with
each other
we were going to do this
and that
but our dreamer died and now we lie here
unattended
unfulfilled
in a wasteland where all hope is gone
and so they died too

death and destruction is all around filling us with
woe
and even joe
is sad and morose
as the light is choked out by the impending darkness
sweeping all over us and

all around us
coming down upon us like a withering frightening
chilling breeze
and causing our hearts to freeze

please joe build us a fire
so we can warm out hands
a fire that we can dance around as we implore the
gods to save us
what a tired and worn out humanity we are
looking at each other with hatred
plotting to kill one another
to stamp out those who disagree with us
or look different than us
or worship a different God than us

where is the love
is it all gone
is only hatred left for us
which leads to violence and destruction

it seems all roads lead to Vegas
escaping is our deep desire
to watch the roulette wheel go round and round
to hear the bell that signifies 10 free spins at the
slots
to hear the slap of the cards at the black jack table
and watch the topless women dance
and eat till we burst
drink till we lose our sense of reality

and fuck till we crash

run away to paradise
where everything is nice
baby let's roll the dice
don't think twice
let's just pay the price
and go

Joe went to the supermarket and pulled down his
pants
he showed his penis to all the people
the people gasped at such a show
and the manager said hey Joe
what's with the show
and Joe
said
let's go
anyone want a piece of this
and everyone ran away frightened by the show
and the cops came and arrested Joe
and put him in jail
and then he went to court and the judge who was a
woman asked him
hey Joe
why the show
and he replied
that his father had just died
and he was feeling down so he went a bit crazy
even as his mind went hazy

the judge gave him a warning and told him not to do
it again
Joe nodded and away he went
a free man again
he went home and built a fire and danced around it
then he cooked a pig and invited his neighbours and
had a big feast

tomorrow is a challenge even as yesterday was
the hope of yesterday is that today is not the end
but a new beginning
as we assault the mountain of our discontent and
find a way to love again
renewing our faith in each other
in God
and in ourselves

amazing grace
is needed for the human race
if we want to get beyond first base
and make a case
to each other's face
that even though we love pink lace
we also need to work hard to be on pace
to win this race
and ace
this trial that we face
to become more than empty space

death is a slap in the face

a chilling reminder of how fragile we are
it scares me to the bone
and makes me want to crumble
and tumble
to the ground in absolute despair
as I walk into my practise room and play Air
from Orpheus on my violin
my fingers shaking on the fingerboard
while horrid scenes of dying play over and over in my
head
wishing that I too was dead

I picked him up from the hospital
a wisp of a man his hair wild and crazy
dressed in hospital pyjamas and only socks on his
feet
and then when we got home we tried to wake him
but he would not open up his eyes
and before we knew it he had passed away
we looked at each other in disbelief
the tears welling up in our eyes
till sobbing and inconsolable we faced the awful
truth
he was gone
gone to who knows where
and in this life we would never see his blessed face
again
or hear his comforting voice
and a great emptiness descended upon us
leaving us scarred forever and desperately sad

Chapter 4

and with this kiss they were wed
so young
and not so strong
but it was only make belief
an act of temporary defiance
stepping outside of the norms for a minute to feel
the power
she said come back to me and my orange crush
and we will drink it together and renew our make
belief vows
he promised he would

us and our world are a collection of atoms stuck
together

with the glue of atomic attraction
and gravity
floating in a sea of ether
our thoughts bouncing off each other in this
cauldron of confusion
trying to find our bearings
what did he mean
why did she say that
how should I react to that
why can't I get any respect
I'm so offended
what should I do
complaining or
explaining
holding onto our jobs
getting better jobs
getting more pay for our work
on and on
minds racing
with jealousy clouding our minds
or inspiring us to do better
to want more
or get even
nightmares
sleeping pills
distractions and hallucinations competing for their
own relevance
finally as we lie on the couch we exhale
and it all comes out
get it out

get it all out

the silence of our thoughts

the violin plays
as the singers voice cuts through the monotony
in the air there is a sense of madness
a lack of control
the weight of the absurdity of the world
falling upon fragile shoulders
sagging
eager faces gazing at the singer
imploring him for guidance
hoping
their hands pressed into each other's
tears in some eyes
smiles on some faces
sad smiles
remembering their own heartaches
their own regrets
their own failures
as the violinist keeps on bowing
the mood so melancholy
and the sad hearts are satisfied

our roads lead back to Warhol
clutching our Polaroid pictures
singing John Lennon songs
and waving in parades

the chandeliers are mocking us
as they hang above our heads
we wander aimlessly in our museums
imagining what was

yesterday knocks at the door
urging us to follow her
and frolic with her on beds of satin
while the wind pounds the rain upon our windows

her perfume seduces the world
as on our knees we beg
for her to stroke our heads
and tell us that it's going to be okay

Chapter 5

morning breaks
she dances on the sea wall
he watches with a muffin in his lap
a cup of coffee in his hands
the sky is blue with some wispy clouds
it could be that perfect day
the one we always dream about
the one we wish would never end
on and on in blissful joy
nothing to do but rest
no work to do today
a spell cast
and a sense of freedom in the air
validation
the universe is backing you up

no thank you
that's what she said from her perch on the couch
smiling sweetly as she taps on her iPad

gethsemane do you matter at all
anymore
they came and arrested him at night
you were there
but where are you now
hiding
sneaking around at the outskirts of Jerusalem
that holy city of God
where angels fought with Satan
as God sought to redeem mankind
in an attempt
to correct
his biggest mistake
saddling the entire human race with eternal
damnation
because
someone ate a fruit after he told them not to
so gethsemane what do you say
let's hear your voice
why do you hide
why can't we find you
why won't you tell us something

the shepherds were keeping their sheep on a hillside
when angels filled the sky and sang for them
Noel

Noel
A king is born
The king of Israel

honesty as seen through a smokescreen
is what I see
as our narcissism shades our perception
and colors our interpretations
is it up
or down
the feeling takes us somewhere
and then we find ourselves standing in a phone booth
wondering
where are we

it's the holidays again and
Johnny is standing alone in Tennessee
wondering if auntie Mabel is going to bring him
some cocaine
he was dreaming of nice straight lines
with sunshine streaming through his windows
a million ways to lose your mind
home sweet home
and a belt of whiskey to set the record straight

the folklore of the partridge in the pear tree was a
comfort
hearts torn apart with grief
losing a loved one
where oh where did you go

to France
with ants in your pants
eating a German schnitzel while trying to dance
it's really up in the air
as are our convictions
torn apart and waiting for inspiration
touch me and make me feel good
she glanced at him provocatively causing more than a
shudder
and then walked away with narry a backwards glance

Ann Frank was a book we read in school
I never believed a word of it
and I told the teacher
what he exclaimed
it's true
is it also true that you Herr Teacher are an imbecile
why you why you go to the principles office
no
what
no you big dick
how dare you
get out get out at once
gladly Herr Hitler
by now he was frothing at the mouth and I
laughing and happy as could be
Anne Frank being true
I couldn't believe how naive
some people will believe anything that's in a book
if it's written it must be true

next we will believe in ufo's
and let's not forget that many of us believe in a god
named YHWH
I prefer Zeus
he seems much more real and logical
but each to their own

some people prefer to go Kung Fu dancing
all night long
finding passionate companions
sharing the joy of the chop chop

behind the old bowling alley
past the pub
he was playing his guitar on the corner and singing

ghosts float effortlessly in the night air
as the sticks keep the beat going
and Irene is drinking sweet Jamaican rum and
dancing with Fred on the street
sweet Jane is playing
and it sounds so sweet
wonder if Anne Frank would like the song
and would she dance to it
or would she turn up her nose and be dismissive

no one likes someone who doesn't believe popular
stories
it's true
it's absolutely true

how can we be so sure
everyone believes so I should to
I don't think so
I can choose to not believe
that's my right in this land of freedom
so stop the bullying
and twisting my arm
I'll believe what I want
and reject what I want
it's my right
it's my privilege
it's my destiny
It's antisemitic to not believe what Anne Frank wrote
why
I don't need to believe
that doesn't make me anything other than a person
who doubts
I can doubt anything I want to
like evolution
like the bible
like the earth is round
it's my right
right or wrong I can think freely
so back off and
bugger off
and quit picking on me because I'm different and
believe differently and
think differently and
act differently
some people like tattoos

I like tattoos
they're sexy and nice and beautiful and expressive
leave people alone to be themselves and quit trying
to process them like
cheese or Bologna or a tin of sardines
we don't belong in labelled boxes
I don't like all the bullies trying to make me think
like them
I like being free
our constitution defends our right to be free
we must be free
we ought to be free
we shall be free

Chapter 6

she held a gun to his head
and shot him in his bed
dead
lock her up they cried
she shot a man and he died
but they set her free
to be
all that she
could be
the times are changing
cover up your eyes
the jokes on you
as you carry your placards on the city streets
and weep
because the past is gone and a new age is upon us

where love reigns
and criminals are forgiven
and jails are banned
and persecution is VERBOTTEN
and the shooting never stops

Chapter 7

I've never been to Berlin
the glory of its history inspires me
I want to know its soul
it's essence
to taste the flavour that it has
to touch it's people
oh Berlin who are you that I can hear your voice
across the ocean
calling to me to come
your arms are wide open as are
the legs of your prostitutes
whose gaze is seductive and mischievous
their bright red lips an inspiration to all who love
living

and want to create a new world
free from worry and free from war and free from
stress and free
free free free
wir lieben die Freiheit
the wall is gone and with it
the definition of who we are
or were
and now- what will we be
us Berliners who've never been there
we can only dream and theorize
and wonder as we applaud the sincerity of our own
lust for knowing
hoping to find what makes us all tick
and seeking an explanation of why we are so thick
as sick
with our own tired schtick
we fight off depression and stick
our heads into darkened corridors where we can sense
life is more absurd than ours
and we crave that depravity
and we crave to know the animal within
and feel the power and the spiritual intuitiveness that
comes from disassociating ourselves from reality
with all our might we want to shout heil
but we bite our tongues and walk slowly and silently
in single file
chanting our own slogans and praying for a sign to
guide us on our way

Chapter 8

the scars of yesterday's kisses
won't heal
why did she steal
a portion of my soul
to sell to the devil
and now the shadows fall
upon my reflection
as I stagger under this heavy load
that I bear
and who gives a care
the Renaissance passed me by
so I sit and cry
and ask why
why Jesus
why me

save me lord
forgive my sins
and set me
free

it's symbolic to assume that everything has a
meaning
what kind of rituals will they use
to where will their spiritualism take them
witch doctors are casting their spells

waiting for salvation on a railway track
jumping off when the train comes by
choo choo
throwing rocks at the hydro line insulators
target practise
sometimes
a spark
then the caboose
and in the bar the people are loose
drinking does that
put on your hat
listen to the beat and dance
as you wonder where you're going
and who you've become
will you get to the kingdom
and get a high five from a King
after this bloody mess
you'd better confess
get on your knees

beg for mercy

sorry lord
for playing the wrong chord
I tried to be free
but ended up in the wrong key
now the dissonance is ringing in my ear
and Alice has a tear
in her eyes
cause the music was such a surprise
taking rebellion to a whole new level
startling the priests who were masterbating in the
belfry
where father Amadeus got his dick caught in
Francis's zipper

watch out
watch out
the witch came in from the back
all dressed in black
displaying a lack
of good graces and a knack
for scaring people out of their wits as she gives them
a wack
on their heads as they lie on a sack
and they
jump up and run away
straight into the arms of monsters who are waiting
their faces grotesque and ugly
and they scream

and they shake
and they shudder

this ambivalent state of affairs is turning heads
a catastrophe is brewing
even as God is stewing
in heaven
the theology which I invented is being
misrepresented
the poets are turning it into a cesspool of slander
and profanity
they've gotten carried away with their sense of logic
and it's diabolic and wrong

Tom said that reality is for people who can't face
drugs
that's a distorted version of religion
without invoking a higher power
or rattling off a million hail mary's
Hail Mary full of grace
what race
do you like the best
and are they from the west
or the east
living with the beast
who drinks mouthwash instead of coffee
turpentine instead of tea
just to make a point
and feel reality

reality lives in an attic
with the ghost of Elvis
and they get along just fine

reality cannot exist within itself
it will suffocate
collapsing in the vacuum of its twisted image
reflected in the mirror of time
with Einstein holding a gun to its head
with the wind swirling dust around the image
with Hollywood holding its side in laughter
reaching hands back to Ginsberg
who was still smiling and reading his poetry

please pass the cornmeal porridge
I like it with my toast
and turn up the radio
open up the curtains
let the sunshine in
and let's stop the crying
and the sighing
and let's stop buying
all the lies fed to us
by the politicians and their accomplices
the rich and the privileged and the judges
dam the judges
they sleep with each other
conniving to deceive the public
plotting to abuse and bully the people
picking on the poor and the destitute and the

underprivileged
please pass the cornmeal porridge
and dam the judges
dam their hypocricy
and dam their lies
they abuse their power daily
when will it end
when will we mend
the system and bend
the rules so that we can send all judges to prison
forever and ever amen

Chapter 9

you who are weary and worn out and
ready and able to throw in the towel
to walk away and leave it all behind
tired of the endless worry and abuse

when will the stress of living ever end and who will
walk beside us
where are the helping hands we need
so tired and so depleted we cry abba father
but no one hears or comes
and we sink to the ground in agony
our spirits kaput and broken
help we sigh
help we cry
why

a child is not a child for 20 years
it remains a child forever and ever
we are all of us children
and we need to be cared for
forever and ever amen

independence is an illusion
taken from the witches brew and transformed into
nonsense
where algebra changes into a dance
and we all prance
to the beat of hysterical drummers
beating skins and wood and water
slashing our way to the primitive jungle that lives in
our minds
where modern technology doesn't exist
and the women beat the clothes at the edge of the
river

wir bleiben Kinder
Papa und Mama wo seit ihr
bitte komm und helfe mir
ich bin verloren in diese große Welt
ich finde nicht mein weg
und ich bin so traurig

Adolph mixed his interpretation of freedom with a
bit of hatred
and raised armies to conquer Europe and beyond
the people were enthralled and scared

finally succumbing to his charm
it was a shameful journey and the price was steep
Berlin finally lay defeated in ruins and the people
gasped at its dethroning
and I who was not yet born never even blinked an eye
I was in the dark
couldn't even grasp the significance of what
happened
but slowly as I lived I began to understand and it was
then as a Berliner that I hung my head in shame
we all hung our heads in shame
and gasped in horror at what we'd all done
even those of us who weren't even there
we all took a share of the blame
spreading it out among us as if we were creating a
peanut butter sandwich
and then breaking bread together like brothers and
sisters

independence is a sin
a protest against the gods
a repudiation of all that is good

the hermits slink back into the Schwarzwald like
cowards
sneaking back into their huts and caves
muttering as they go
strange creatures who defy the rules of the game and
dare to abandon mankind

what is known is repudiated
and that which is unknown becomes the gospel
as mysteries collide with invented reality
showering our consciousness with fables and lore
the past continually haunting us as it stands on the
corner and preaches
and reaches
out to us and beyond
grasping us in its gnarled hands and demanding we
adhere to its laws

daring to defy the ancient customs Eli hummed his
own tune
going his own way
alone
paying the price with loneliness and rejection
finally returning to the fold
in from the cold
and no more so bold

she stood crying on the corner
and he knew she was downsick again
so much pain
and nothing to gain
so he gave her ten bucks
and crossed himself and walked away
he was a priest and he was gay
what was he to say
to a lady who was not okay
lost in a pharmaceutical world today

tormented by memories of sadness and depression
broken to pieces

how can we mend this broken heart
where would we even start
to heal the wounds so deep and raw
where everything is a last straw
threatening to completely destroy the fragile person

and you think that Rasputin is dead
but like Jesus he rose again
and whispers secrets to his chosen few
his disciples who hang onto his every word
wanting to please their master
and convert the world to his way of thinking
they hide behind the Kremlin walls
and plot a way to rule the world
they have fellow conspirators in Berlin who
are inspired by the words they say
lead us oh Rasputin they beseech
show us the way
hitler was a fraud and now we search for truth
and turn away from all things uncouth
those terrible things that hitler taught us
we look for light
not might
we look for hope
not dope
we look for a shiny new car
not tar

Chapter 10

I am committed not to the rules of this society
but to an institute
in an abstract sense
the same place Einstein went to invent his silly
notions of gravity
anything can be made to look logical when you fool
yourselves in an abstract environment
keep on rocking as you smoke your pot
turn up the music as you turn off your mind
become a victim and cry till you die
poor so and so
poor poor victim
bury them in a garbage can
worthless

he won the jackpot
she danced on the terrace
together they flew into outer space
they laughed at their good fortune
it seemed so mythical
so out of order
like playing in an orchestra on a grassy knoll

sail captain sail
and mind your beeswax

love has no patience
it is pushy and impertinent and combatitive
and won't take no for an answer
love doesn't hang like an invisible thing in the air

into the night they danced
and drank cognac
as the greenbacks rained down on their parade

it's madness in this world
clowns dancing on our beds
ballerinas playing cello in the parlour
aunt Betty cooking goats head soup
while uncle Herbert takes a poop
under the pear tree in the front yard
with the neighbours looking on
gasp gasp
and then along comes Jezebel wearing Italian jeans
everyone blushes

the nonsense fills the air
as we all dance about without a care
pretending that the world is wonderful

the full moon shone in the morning sun
glowing in a bright sky
and I keep driving along in my baby blue Chevy
I turn the corner
the billboard says for sale
and in my mind I buy
sold cries out the auctioneer
sold to the man in the baby blue Chevy
I glance in my rear view mirror
on a flat deck truck a woman is playing the
saxophone
I thought it very strange
out here on the range
but I drove on
after all
it was a mad world

the siren wails and the cop pulls over the Chevy
speeding buddy
here's your ticket
obey the rules or else

I went to school
to learn a rule
or two
so I could exist in this primitive society

and learn how not to be free

don't do this
don't do that
don't do anything at all
just sit there and be quiet
become invisible and fade away
and another thing
wear this straight jacket to bed

twinkle twinkle little jerk
off you go to work
make your mamma proud and be a slave

Chapter 11

unkempt hair and broken shoelaces
sullen faces and ripped up pants
and she rants
and rages as she struts along the street complaining
blaming
all she meets for all the woes

er hat seinen engeln befohlen
bitte retten sie die Menschheit
so verloren sind sie alle

lost lost lost
in this sea of melancholy desperation where we fight
and claw our way forward
daring to put it all on the line

even agreeing to pay a fine
for breaking rules so we can
get
to
the
head
of
the Line

follow me all ye sheep and dare not to question my
place at the head of the line
it was my destiny
all in the master plan by you know who
who said
thou oh great and noble one you shall lead
and others shall follow
and that is the attitude of all who lead

together we fall except for the rich who retire to
their mansions
where they have hoarded all manners of luxuries
there they laugh and
play
and make fun of the rest of us poor peasants
but then sometimes the peasants are mad
and they break into the mansions and kill the rich
and take all their stuff
and declare that a revolution is breaking out
and the world turns a new leaf
where the poor become the rich

but
without money or fame or class
although some demand that others lick their ass
and nothing really changes but the players

die Menschheit so verloren
so kaputt

Karl Marx only wanted to bring people together
equality was his thing
this great German philosopher who got lost in
England
it was the yang to his yin
the tension was too great
and he collapsed as his ideas burst into flames
igniting a bomb
which exploded
and killed so many innocent lives

gib mir deine hand
zusammen wollen wir gehen in diesen leben
ich liebe dich
und du liebst mich

as he ate the crust
he wondered if he could trust
society to have his back
and not give him a wack
as he lay sleeping in his bed
and make him dead

Chapter 12

so many rules
and so many schools
teach the children to obey
so that they never go their own way

Molly cared
so she dared
to break away
and kill the man who abused her
and now the system abuses her
rules and rules
and more rules and rules
thou shalt not kill
but please feel free to take all the abuse that bullies
put on you

after all we are free to do as we please unless we
defend ourselves
and then
rules and rules and rules

if someone hits you do not turn the other cheek
hit them back harder
that's the golden rule
Jesus lost his way
or should we say
the scribes lied about it all
evolution is a bitch

where is the composition of order
lying within the negative space of our souls
where magnetism overrides the existing creation
a stunted evolution that refuses to grow
but in the end
the show must go on
and the rules are incidental
waiting on us
like waiters
more coffee mam

over in the next room the painter is having a
meltdown
the colours are denying the existence of order
without rules they run everywhere
helter skelter
out of control

like a society that hangs it's lawgivers and
rips its constitution into pieces
burning them in a huge bonfire
as the townspeople come and watch
wringing their hands
pressing their lips together
and staring reluctantly into the fire

dark is the night
without light
and scary with robbers hiding in bushes and behind
trees
plotting to rob the people or kill them
taking their money and jewelry
and hurting them in the process
call the police
come and help the people
who will help the people
who will defend the people
laws are being broken and people are being robbed
society is crumbling as we give in to our anarchaic
tendencies
freedom what is it good for if we all die
freedom what is it good for if we all cry
freedom what is it good for if none of us gets to eat
our pie

the doctor has prescribed a disease for me
that way I can stay in bed
acting like I'm dead

it's my excuse to withdraw from life
it tires me out to be so sedentary

paradise and the cult of pleasure
opens up bewildering vistas
that inspire
after you tire
of the obvious and predictable
and you are drowning in a sea of boredom
help me
save me
I'm drowning in a sea of mediocrity
kick me if you have to
out of this comfortable bed that I'm dying in
taking all those barbiturates
deadening my senses
please open up the window and let the birds fly in
be my Jesus and save me from this death

parasites are crawling around in the playgrounds of
the judicial societies
eating away at the little semblance of honesty and
integrity that is left
zombies are knocking on the door
crying out loud and begging
let us in
but the door is bolted shut
as are the taps of creativity
deep in the confusion about right and wrong
is a joker with snakes crawling at his feet

crouched and ready to spring
and get into the ring
with the grotesque witch from Harvard
we know everything
we are the best
we rule
the joker laughs - what fools
and falls on the ground as the blood runs from his
mouth

Chapter 13

in New York City the roses bloom
as in the alleys the big guns boom
everywhere you feel the gloom
the people there are full of doom

New Yorkers act like they love to hate
they don't like intercourse they just masterbate
they'd rather kick you than be nice
and all their hair is filled with lice

cockroaches and anger fill their spaces
of love and kindness there are no traces
all they think about is making money
they got no time for peaches and honey

they're so dumb they think they're cool
when really they just play the fool
acting like their shit don't stink
and playing with their neighbours dink

New York City is a giant slum
and everyone there is a smelly bum
what a lousy place to live
the people there have nothing to give

Chapter 14

when Elvis walked in Berlin
he walked alone at night
his blue suede shoes on the cobblestones
dreaming of Memphis
and Graceland
the ghost of Adolph walking beside him
wearing sunglasses
reminiscing with clenched teeth
he shouted at Elvis
forgive me Elvis
but Elvis could not see or hear him
he just kept on walking
many people have seen Elvis after he died
I'm not one of them

in the ghetto they fought with knives
suspicious minds in a rage
wanting to protect their turf or
take over someone else's
lebensraum

Chapter 15

St.Peter is sitting at the gates to heaven
beautiful golden gates inset with pearls and
diamonds
he sits on a throne made of silver and gold
and on his head is a crown of unequalled splendour

St.Lucifer sits at the gates to hell
dark and foreboding gates made of R-bar and
platinum
he sits on a throne made of cast iron and diamonds
and on his head is a crown of unequalled spendour

the people approach the gates with apprehension
clutching their sins and good deeds in their hands
it takes a lot of good deeds to get into heaven

it takes a lot of sins to get into hell

sorry not enough good deeds
sorry not enough sins
where to now
no one wants this one

many live in no-mans land between the two
kingdoms
their so-so lives did not entitle them to either land
they languish in the wilderness where there is no
judge
and no Saviour

Chapter 16

the news was sad again
the world was still insane
the people seemed to have gone mad
it all made me feel so bad

opening the curtains I saw it was a sunny day
and I thought everything would be okay
there is bad and there is good
I'd make it all good if I could

after a day of work
and feeling like a guy named dirk
I wanted to walk on the wild side
to swim against the tide

sometimes I feel like I'm just hanging on
and everyone around me is in on some kind of con
tricking me and laughing at me
what a way to be

oh well what can I do
but go to the loo
go to the park
kiss a hooker after dark
take a trip to Paris or Rome
or play tennis in a great big dome

sometimes I get so bored
I want to cut the cord
and fly away into outer space
becoming a basket case

I love to go and see a movie
something very groovy
and eat some popcorn and drink some coke
and hope that I don't choke

then I'll go to bed and dream
of eating peaches and cream
and I would get up at noon
listening to a nice rock and roll tune

Chapter 17

how can you be a Berliner if you've never been to
Berlin
that is the question
the big fat question
in the end we are what we are
what we believe in
how we see ourselves
and others can criticize
and put us down
and tell us we don't matter and we can't be who we
are
but we know who we are
and we don't need to let them put us down or tell us
who we are
so many want to lord it over us

and teach us to believe in their way
but we don't want to believe in their way
we want to go our own way
nonconforming
rebels
outcasts

I see the gates of the city
I am filled with joy
it is my city
it is my Berlin
it is my solace

die haben mir gefragt
kanst du deutsch reden
und ich habe geantwortet ya
ganz unbedingt spreche ich Deutsch
daß ist meine Muttersprache
daß war meine erste Sprache

my dad fought in the German army in the Second
World War
that didn't make him a Nazi
he was a soldier
he did his duty
he wasn't evil like hitler
he was just a soldier
obey your superiors and fight
fight or be killed
survival

don't judge me
don't judge my father
quit throwing stones at us

I have chosen to be a Berliner
it's a choice for some of us
and where is the sin in that
don't throw your stones at me
build a fire pit with your stones
make a nice fire and roast a pig
have a feast and invite your friends
drink a toast to a wonderful world full of kindness
and love

John Fitzgerald Kennedy stood in Berlin and said
ich bin ein Berliner
I stand in Vancouver and say
ich bin ein Berliner

Chapter 18

she threw all the crusts from her blueberry toast into
the blue bowl
there she said and
waved her hand in the air
she was a tease
and the clown had his heart broken
in the end it was only a game
what a shame
and now the clown has a frown
he feels so down
as he shuffles down the street

those unfaithful wretches
chasing every skirt
playing around in the dirt

like naughty children
what will mother say
bad boy you did not obey
and now everyone has to pay for all that infidelity
for that lack of sincerity
for the absence of respect
lass mich fliegen in meine Träume
bitte mein Gott
ich will zum Himmel fliegen
to find pure beauty
and touch the perfect body
are we freaks
or monsters who've lost their way
who
look in the broken mirror
do you recognize your heartbreak
is it really you
or an impression
an interpretation of a younger you
wistful eyes looking at you beseechingly
and you wonder
is it a stranger
lost in this universe of pain
where planets spin and spin and spin
and then I noticed the piano player quietly playing in
the corner
he was naked
and there was a naked girl sitting next to him
sometimes whispering in his ear
and then he would nod or shake his head

and this went on for the entire evening
around two in the morning they left
we kept on drinking and then we too went home
I think it was around six in the morning
and when I went to bed I had many dreams

counterculture depravity has us all fooled
as we fool around and experiment with this and that
the thrills
and the pills to enhance our pleasure and call it
enlightenment
trips that yield inner trauma and make us question
our sanity
are we increasing our intellectual prowess
are we increasing our creativity
are we increasing our emotional fortitude
we shudder on a philosophical level as we slide down
so many slippery slopes
our hands flailing about trying to latch onto
something
to grasp an element of stability even as we fall
recklessly
in this vacuum of uncertainty that we've created
that our professors created
that our politicians created

scary monsters leave me alone
go back to your studies at the university and quit
trying to scare me

mathematical theories define the abstract notions
that the inventor has
he works into the night trying to come to grips with
his insanity
his endless desire to find answers within the bubble
he's created
in the morning he takes out his paintbrush and
paints a series of circles
a red one
a blue one
a yellow one
then he goes to sleep on his couch as the music of
Bowie plays

restlessness tosses us from side to side
if only we could concentrate
focus man
focus

the Berlin philharmonic is my fave
of them I rant and rave
I've watched them play
what can I say
not in person but on the Internet
so don't fret
please eat your Apple streudel and give love a chance
then you can prance
about in your panties so pink
and not make a stink
about the fact

that the Nazis made a pact
with Karajan and kept him safe from harm
even as he put on the charm
with a baton that was so restless and full of life
in that time of murder and strife

sie schläft im Grunewald
aber ich weiß daß sie wandert hier und da
manchmal kann man ihr singen hören
auf die Straßen in Berlin oder
New York City
she was so fine
but she will never be yours or mine

roses in a vase on my bookcase
standing there with my books on Jesus
like they know something
something about crucifixions and love
it's the beauty in the old old story
hence Magdalene
and she wasn't the only groupie
flowers are natures gift
an answer to pain

then the door flies open and Santa Claus jumps in
where the hell is my milk and cookies
and everyone looks at him in surprise
where he bellows
and they shrug their shoulders
why would we give you milk and cookies

because it's tradition you dumb asses
security comes and drags the guy out of there
what was that asks the poducer
and everyone looks at him with blank stares

that's just it
no one knows shit
they just wander about
and cringe when someone lets go of a shout
security takes away the bad guy and it's over
next

Chapter 19

waiting at the edge for someone
holding up her mirror
wondering
who will show some love
how will they kiss
if they kiss at all
or will they all walk by
she goes to the circus and watches the clowns
and buys some popcorn
standing at the entrance she waits
for someone
wanting to put her arms around someone
and feel something
she looks in the mirror
and likes what she sees

so she walks away
with autumn leaves falling around her
as she walks to her home
in Berlin

a philosopher rakes up his leaves
what does he find
more leaves
he rakes them all into a pile and then lights them on
fire
it smells good
burning leaves in fall
another philosopher comes and stands beside him
together they watch the leaves burn
nice fire
ya I like the smell
and all your leaves are gone
ya all gone
isn't that nice
ya so nice let's go in and have a beer
ya that's a good idea
they go in and have a couple of beers and watch some
football
then they order in pizza and have more beers
after the game the guest goes home
and the leaf raker goes to bed and falls asleep
he dreams of raking up leaves and making a fire
in the morning he gets up and eats some Cheerios
then he goes to work at the university and lectures
on philosophy

meanwhile in Berlin she goes to bed and has a good
sleep
dreaming of her imaginary lover

Andy was mysterious because he was so honest
we don't know how to deal with truth
we run from it
pretend it doesn't exist
bury it in textbooks about philosophy and poetry
such a pretentious lie
Andy was not a pretender even though it appeared he
was
taking Polaroids to expose immediate reality
he was a great philosopher
and who knows
he might have been her imaginary lover
or a leaf raker in another lifetime

look into the mirror
what do you see
are you a mystery or
simply mysterious

he languished in the white room
pacing his room like a caged animal
full of psychedelic melancholy and pain
and dreaming dreams
where red and white birds flew into the sun
where the mountaintops were covered in maraschino
cherries

where witches flew around in brooms made of black
Licorice
where chocolate covered peanuts covered
Mt.Olympus
where an orchestra played in a walnut grove
where a choir sang up in the sky in a balloon which
drifted westward

uniformity can steal our individuality
it's a rebellion against loneliness
but underneath it all we crave excitement
we lust for sexual pleasure and power to be ourselves
without society demanding that we conform
do this or else
what
are you kidding
I don't believe this
come on
that's not the way we do it here
okay

skinny girls are so dam sexy
a reflection of purity
femme fatale is in the house and she jumps on the
couch
and down again
up and down
we should all reinvent ourselves many times to keep
from getting bored
and offer ourselves up as museum installations

so others could examine us and interpret our features
transformative art

who is she
who are you
what does he want here
who is doing your hair for the ball
wasn't her hair just divine
and those shoes - to die for
talk about an exciting perfume
and then she walked into the living room wearing
nothing but sunshine
and a pink g-string
the people just stared
and she smiled and giggled
so they all smiled and giggled too

hearts half empty
as bad memories seep in
starving the soul
and making it shudder
inferiority complex
if only I could look like so and so
to be beautiful
to be loved
to be respected
how can I change myself
plastic surgery perhaps
but then
so what

do I get cold and quiet
sitting in corners by myself
nibbling on cheese and crackers
bemoaning my lack of social graces
confused and humiliated
forgotten and forsaken
disrespected and ignored

they thought it was a precious pearl
but it was only a factory girl
dancing topless on the boulevard
and acting like a card

Chapter 20

he sat at the table
with his dear auntie Mable
eating his curds and whey

then along came the Don
dear old uncle John
who sat down and ate some toast

his friend Laura Jane
who was certifiably insane
also claimed a seat with them all

then along came Frank and Joe and Pete
all taking their seat
and eating some steak and eggs

it was a nice little party
then don made a farty
and everyone booed in disgust

then auntie Mable pulled out a gun
and said hey hon
how about a game of Russian roulette

so they all took turns with the gun at their head
and finally someone was dead
as the bullet entered the brain

and so it was that uncle John died
and everyone at the table cried
and vowed never to play Russian roulette again

Chapter 21

they built a house on lot 28
and the walls were not even straight
Tom went back there many times and never got done
or so it seemed
and it depressed him
it had a big living room
and slatted boards around the fireplace
with ugly black brick at the entry
it was a nightmare on lone oak street
where ghosts and ghouls would congregate and play
poker at night
you could hear them screaming when they lost money

Tom went and moved to the moon
he lived there with his pet raccoon

who looked like a goon
Tom was a bit of a loon
who loved sex at noon
but mostly came too soon
all the while whistling a happy tune

the boxer lived in New York City
he was friends with a stripper named Loretta
together they went to plays
together they drank coffee
together they flew over the moon

a private oasis is what we want
where we can rest and think our own thoughts
no one to judge us or
cast upon us their dispersions
there are no nightmarish expectations
and no bells and whistles to call us to service

Chapter 22

the storm is coming
run baby run
into the arms of love
the bad man held up the bank
frightening the tellers
who gave him all their money
he put it in his bag and ran away
run baby run
into the arms of love
a cup of coffee to calm the nerves
it's a cruel world
where bad men lie in wait to victimize and kill
run baby run
into the arms of love

Chapter 23

I imagine that the glamorous women in Berlin would
cast a spell on me
and I would sink lower and lower
finally lying on the ground
help me
help me

in eine fantasiewelt geh ich
da freut die Ameise sich
zusammen haben wir eine gute zeit
so eine schöne gelegenheit
und wir tanzen
und wir singen
und wir trinken

he stood in the living room beside the big red
painting
dreaming of his laboritory
aufwiedersehn meine freunde
he could hear the words echoing in his head
and the shrill voice of the stranger asking about
ideology
such a superfluous denunciation
why bow down to the authorities
giving them control over your thoughts
surrender
why
the option is disobedience and risking punishment
years in the slammer
years under the hammer
well dam her
just do it and don't let her dictate your life
but then the repercussions are too much and
the new perspective will become a dangerous point of
view
giving rise to slogans
meaningless pieces of unnecessary hype

and again walking in Berlin after dark
sacred streets with hidden meanings
buildings leaning in to tell you secrets

gib mir gelt
die Menschheit bittet

transitions to otherworldly corridors beckon
they stand in stark contrast to existing and
acceptable procedures
where is peace
where is free speech
why the tape over our mouths

and so he became like the others
solitary creatures scared to say anything at all
it was pragmatic to be quiet
and with the silence the inspiration was gone
such a tragedy
as the city clerks trespassed on our rights and drove
our spirits into the ground

we took trips but someone took down all the signs
it was no wonder we're all lost
looking for our flavour
what flavour is in anyways
und wo ist die Ordnung
wir wissen nicht
they accuse us of fascism if we want laws
they accuse us of communism if we want to help each
other
they accuse us of anarchy if we want freedom

the monks call us to worship
walking slowly behind each other chanting
their eyes cast to the ground
their hands clutching their crucifixes

praying to the god they cannot see but hope
he is there
the God of Abraham and of Moses and of Jesus

she tries on a new dress
how do you like it
I don't know
another one
how about this one
I think it suits you
really
why
I don't know but I feel it
okay I will take it

Chapter 24

der Untergrund
wo die nagte frauen spielen
da schlägt Mo auf die trammeln
und das Lied Sweet Jane spielt eviglich
hier wird himmlischer Wein von gut-aussehenden
männern serviert
und Bilder des großen New Yorkern Philosophen Lou
Reed hängen an die wänden
no bright lights
no flying kites
just a collection of dreamers
plotting to take over the world
over cigarettes wine and song

we need to be replanted many times
like the lily
to gain stature
flavour
sweet and bitter
full of love and hate and bitterness and sweetness
and regret and kindness and pride
changing
evolving
becoming real people as we experience pain and
misery and sorrow
we suffer
we triumph
we die

under the streets of Berlin he also died
even as above a nation cried
going from victor to vanquished
from pride to shame
such desolation
such deep deep sorrow
it's response to its harsh and barbarian treatment by
others deemed too much
as it fought for justice and lebensraum
against nations who had bullied and intimidated it
nations who had sought to embarrass and destroy its
soul
turning its people into slaves and servants
it was too much
there had to be a reaction

what did they expect
a proud and strong nation cannot be subjugated
it will rise from the ashes and take its revenge
again and again and again

franky told a story
about war and love and glory
I am not mad
he cried as they told him he was bad
don't make me sad
he cried as he decried the latest fad
which was to intimidate those who still loved the
führer
I am free to love those I want to
what should I do
give in to your propaganda and join the ranks of the
haters
those who denounce the nation
and bring shame upon our heads
making us weep upon our beds
traitors lie in wait at every corner
their knives sharp
their tongues sharper
their loyalty wavering like a candle in the wind

what should they do then
who can they turn to
all the candy taken away
and sentenced again to lives of sadness and sorrow
their spirits squashed like an ant beneath the tires of

a car
still from the ghettos of yesterday we hear the
screams
as we cover up our ears
wanting to eat our cake in silence
and drink our coffee in peace
to stop being reminded of the tragedy and move on
to feel the sun upon our faces
and let it burn away all traces
of the horror that we were a part of

the cure is all in the medicine
a needle here and an operation there
coming for you joe
your sickness has gone too far
do you have a pulse
could it be that you are dead already
and your spirit is escaping
quick grab a net
catch him before he flies away
bring him back

she stood in the living room and conducted an
imaginary orchestra
until the bassoonists stood up and walked out
what now
the violin section threw down their instruments
and the guest conductor threw a tantrum
she broke down in tears
mommy help me

the case
can be made that looking into space
and dreaming of infinity is an indication that there
are psychedelic memes
living beyond the moon
waiting for astronauts
and also cartoonists

it's an accidental incident of fashionable hysterics
preying on the young fashion conscious artists
who when slashing their canvasses
and burning their brushes
pray to the Mona Lisa
to open their eyes and teach them how to be true
artists
revellence seems beyond their grasp
even as they clasp
their hands together in desperation and despair
fearing rejection and heartless criticism

reality is conjecture
spinning forever within the fundamental principles
that define anti-matter
elusive thoughts cannot gain a foothold and
therefore spin out of control
careening on this highway of theories
unproven and untested beyond their abstract
environment

Chapter 25

if you want to go to heaven
which heaven is that
and can you bring your cat
or your baseball bat
will the Beatles be there or
what about the Velvet Underground
or do you opt for all those virgins
endless sex and pleasure

God only knows
Zeus or Poseidon or Yahweh or Baal
which one do you choose
which one is the true God
which one is real

he was a slave to love
rescue me
she was abused by her lover
rescue me
they tried every position under the sun
rescue me

freedom cries in the corner after being flogged by the
mayor
how dare you lay a whipping on freedom
freedom does as she pleases
whenever she pleases
however she pleases
she is free to be free

take your chains and hang them on a hook in your
garage

in the acid rain we walked
all night we talked
our tears fell together on the asphalt
around us the buildings rose
up to the sky
blocking the light
from the moon
which was full
in the club the lead guitar was soaring
the drummer was beating his skins to death
through the smoky window we could see the crowd
dancing

our souls reached out to each other
we kissed in the shadow of a green dumpster

follow the arrows
they lead you to
the promised
land

what's going on
are you distracted
looking for clues in the firmament
searching for keys to yourself

the guarantees were useless
who has the authority to grant them
like a trap
and then - it's all over
darkness and eternal servitude
beware of the promises made by silver tongued
smiley people
don't trust the smiley people
with their eternal optimism and fair weather ways
their smiles are an illusion
as they cover up their wickedness and backstabbing
characters
put your faith in no one
put your trust in no one
put your foot through the wall and curse the smiley
faces
they win your trust and then they destroy you

like a wagon full of whores who entice
and then they strike
and then they don't know you anymore
like a lure hiding a hook they seek to win you over
and then
beat you over the head and rob you

smoking crack
around the track
baby come back
into the sack
are you Mack
no I'm Jack
and I have a knack
for knowing how to quack
like a duck who's out of wack

Chapter 26

I have heard about the autobahn
about no speed limits and
people smashing themselves and others to death
riding in their fancy fast cars and throwing caution
to wind
fast and faster and faster
it's out of control
someday I hope that I will see it
to drive upon it
and feel the glory of its decadence
opening up the windows of my auto to feel the
wind

we want to do better
to be greater

inventing amazing things
going into outer space and conquering distant
galaxies
we dream of Starwars and extratestrial beings
piloting our sleek and fast rockets to the corners of
our universe
stand not in our way oh ye of little faith
and even less fortitude
don't hinder us in our push for success and speed
and glory
timidness has no place with us
we are the family of man and we are pioneers
we are adventurers
we are conquistadors

I love to eat cake on Sunday morning
sipping my cappuccino slowly
trying to make the time go slowly
and she walks by my window
wearing furs and a diamond necklace
I go back to bed
dreaming in technicolor
and I'm walking in Berlin
and all around people are walking around naked
with tattoos of Elvis on their asses
a policeman offers me a doobie
I decline cause I'm thinking
this is a trap
he gives me the Nazi salute
and walks away

a priest gives me a can of sardines opened up and a
fork
and I eat it
then I wake up and go back to my cake
taking another bite
yum

truth stands on the corner and masterbates
but it never comes
and as it beats itself off a crowd gathers
they cheer truth on
come on truth you can do it
and truth tries but never comes
finally truth gives up and walks away
the crowd stays
and wonders
what now

chapman shot Lenin
and he died
it was unexpected
why
what a stupid thing to do
mad people disrupt the world and we can't stop them
we only react after the fact
senseless acts of violence are pissing me off
dam those assholes
disrespecting their own freedom
such a precious thing
and so easily abused

no one is amused
except sometimes the accused
and we pat them on the shoulder and say poor dear
must have had a rough childhood
must have had some mental challenges
must been addicted to something
except if it's your own family member who gets
shot
then you want to shoot the murderer in retaliation
dam
and you're so mad
so pissed off
so hurt
and you feel so powerless
so hopeless
and so utterly mad

alles ist gut
lass uns ein schönes lied singen
und tanzen
lass uns alles einfach machen
eine neue zeit kommt
die Zukunft ruft uns an
what was the journey like
over the mountains
across rivers
and then finally sitting at a table in Copenhagen
counting the wrinkles on my hands
and contemplating starting an art school in Paris
dreaming of abstract art

wanting to express oneself with a paintbrush and a
canvass
in order to capture the essence of our fear of the
uncertainty of the future

Chapter 27

where are you Lady Luck
it's you I want to fuck
to feel myself inside of you and become as one
and when we're done
with our intercourse to kiss you and stroke your head
as you lie beside me in bed
praying that you bless me
praying that you will set me free
praying that you will be
a good luck charm

who's selling his used bike at the crossroads
looks like an old musician
long hair and a headband and tattered Italian jeans
for sale

like new
they turn their heads as they drive past
he lights up a cigarette
cracks open a beer
a corvette stops
a tall blonde steps out
how much
1000.00
okay
she pays him in cash and her friend gets on the bike
and takes off
the old musician gets in the car with her and they
drive off too

we're always selling something
sometimes it's our body
sometimes it's our belongings
sometimes it's our virginity

we are all sellers and buyers
trying to figure out the price
trying to find the value

how much
this much
that much
really
holy cow or
is that all

how much to save mankind from hell
the sacrifice of the son of God
all of mankind
everyone if they accept
and if they don't
let them burn in hell
isn't that just a bit harsh
I love them
you do
I love them
how is that
I love them

the passion was there
everything was on fire
burning
and then it petered out
what happened
what the hell happened
what in gods name happened

deep thinkers we all could be
if only a good education could be had
what about our inherent distorted mental condition
did you see the cuckoo bird fly
to the monastery where all the nuns sigh
as the priests all cry
the pope has abdicated
because he fornicated
and the midnight mass has been cancelled

Rome goes dark
everything is so stark
as over in Berlin the dogs begin to bark

Chapter 28

I never knew him
cock a doodle doo
I never knew him
cock a doodle doo
I never knew him
cock a doodle doo

Chapter 29

Brahms
had no qualms
about destroying his compositions if he didn't like
them
he never realized that perfection is a myth
perpetuated by a narcissistic fantasy
to overthrow the world order
perfection is a disease
a malady of the mind
that can never be cured
only tolerated and despised

be of good cheer
wake up and have a beer
get drunk before noon

and act like a loon
always be late for work
but never act like a jerk

feeling a little seasick
as I reached out my hands
hoping for help
please Jesus
turn this water into wine
take me to a place of everlasting joy
my reason has left me
truth is a stranger
so I huddle under my blanket
with only my hands exposed and outstretched
begging for your blessing
for your kindness
hoping to see your blessed face
smiling at me
please lord
turn this water into wine
so I can drink
and be filled with your power
so this ghastly life can be changed

my pretentiousness is the cloak that I wear
to protect myself and keep the thieves away
those ferocious beasts who seek to plunder and
destroy
they lurk everywhere
trying to destroy me

to attack and vanquish
and so
I run and hide
behind the fashion that I've created
that others have created
and I have appropriated
it's my armour
so please don't expose me
and leave me in danger
let me live
I'd do the same for you
so together we can safely walk
in this world of woe
and find comfort in our masquerade

www.ingramcontent.com/pod-product-compliance
Lightning Source LLC
Chambersburg PA
CBHW031318040426
42443CB00005B/129